The Dark Figure in the Doorway

Books By Morton Marcus

Origins (Kayak, 1969)

Where The Oceans Cover Us
(Capra, 1972)

The Santa Cruz Mountain Poems
(Capra, 1972; Capitola Book Company, 1992)

The Armies Encamped In The Fields Beyond The Unfinished Avenues: Prose Poems
(Jazz Press, 1977)

The Brezhnev Memo
(Dell/Delacorte, 1980) Novel

Big Winds, Glass Mornings, Shadows Cast By Stars: Poems, 1972-1980
(Jazz Press, 1981)

Pages From A Scrapbook Of Immigrants
(Coffee House, 1988)

When People Could Fly: Prose Poems
(Hanging Loose, 1997)

Moments Without Names: New & Selected Prose Poems
(White Pine Press, 2002)

Shouting Down The Silence: Verse Poems 1988-2001
(Creative Arts, 2002)

Pursuing The Dream Bone: New Prose Poems
(Quale Press, 2007)

Striking Through The Masks: A Literary Memoir
(Capitola Book Company, 2008)

— EDITOR —

In A Dybbuk's Raincoat: The Collected Poems of Bert Meyers,
with Daniel Meyers (University of New Mexico Press, 2007)

— TRANSLATOR —

The Star Wizard's Legacy: Six Poetic Sequences By Vasko Popa
(White Pine Press, 2010)

THE DARK FIGURE IN THE DOORWAY

—Last Poems—

Morton Marcus

White Pine Press / Buffalo, New York

Publication of this book was made possible, in part, with public funds from the New York State Council on the Arts, a State Agency.

The author thanks the editors of the following periodicals, where many of these poems first appeared: *Alaska Review:* "Before & After"; Alcatraz: "Goodbye To All That"; *Bloomsbury Review:* "Pavel Tcelichtew's 'Hide and Seek,'" "Silos," "The Gods Are Playing Tennis With Our Lives"; *Brilliant Corners: A Journal of Jazz and Literature:* "Summer, 1953"; *Caesura:* "The Eighth Day"; *El Corno Emplumado:* "The Measure, The Breath"; *Hanging Loose:* "The Man with the Moustache," "Our Neighbor In The Mountains," "Give & Take," "Summer, 1953," "White Castle, 1954," "Listening To Lou Harrison's 'Suite for Violin & American Gamelan,'" "What I Wanted From Women," "Bear Prints;" *Hearse:* "At 31"; *Kayak:* "Wondering"; *Luna:* "Radio," "His First Body"; *Midwest Review:* "Serenade To A Christmas Tree," "New Year's Eve"; *Poetry East:* "At Times I Want To Curse My Words," "Ladybug," "The Boy In The Sandbox," "These Hands," "What Have You Thought About Today?" "At 63," "The Roshi's Reply," "Rejoice with Me," "Snapshot: John Walther Plays The Cello," "Mily Balakirev: A Life In Music," "I Have A Talk With My Body," "The Farm Wife's Dream," "Prayer," "All We Can Do," and "The Village Is Empty"; *Poetry International:* "Living With Su Dong-Po," "The Snow Outside"; *The Prose Poem: An International Journal:* "My Triangle"; *Red Wheelbarrow:* "This Terrible Cold," "The Village Is Empty"; *Sentence 7 & 8:* "Pears," "Navel," "Rocks and Trees," "Paintings," "The First Laugh."

And in the following anthologies: *Revenge and Forgiveness:* "Forgiveness"; *Monterey Bay Anthology:* "All Over The Planet."

Special Thanks to The Prado Museum in Madrid for allowing us to use Diego Velazquez's painting, "Las Meninas," for the book cover.

And, as always, *thanks to my daughter,* Jana, for the tireless work she did on the ms.

First Edition.

ISBN: 978-1-935210-16-0

Printed and bound in the United States of America.

Library of Congress Control Number: 2010925985

White Pine Press
P.O. Box 236
Buffalo, New York 14201
www.whitepine.org

Contents

I. The Eighth Day

II. The Dark Figure In The Doorway

III. All We Can Do

Introduction

PETER JOHNSON

A little over ten years ago, I wrote a review of Morton Marcus' book of prose poems, *When People Could Fly.* At that time I mentioned that it seemed strange to call Mort an underappreciated writer because he had published more than three hundred and fifty verse and prose poems in little magazines, along with seven books of poetry and one novel. Also, his work had been included in over seventy American and international anthologies; and many articles had been written on him and his poetry. He had also penned a theater piece, *The Eight Ecstasies of Yaeko Iwasaki: A Legend in Poetry, Dance, and Music,* which had two successful engagements on the West Coast. Still, at that time, he hadn't received the recognition of some his contemporaries and fellow *Kayak* poets, like Charles Simic and James Tate.

Since then Mort has published four more volumes of poetry, a translation of Vasko Popa's poems, and a fascinating memoir *(Striking Through the Mask)* that no doubt pleased, amused, and maybe even pissed off a lot of contemporary poets. With the publication of his last book, *The Dark Figure in the Doorway,* it's clear that the only way you could be oblivious to Mort's work or to his influence on younger poets, especially prose poets, is if you spent your whole life in a paper bag.

And to those of us who knew Mort well, his life was just as important as his work. In fact, in his case, the two are inseparable. Mort put this final book together shortly before he died, and true to his character, he described his intentions to me, concerned I might not recognize the book's formal and thematic shifts. He pointed out that these poems are a "miscellany" and that his "method of organization was twofold: one poem opens on something (an object or idea) mentioned in the poems before it, and the poems usually make up a group of poems on a particular theme that has preoccupied me in my writing/personal life." Although there is some truth to this analysis, I've always been skeptical of poets' descriptions of their own work, and I would argue that there is something far more profound going on in *The Dark Figure in the Doorway* than even Mort recognized, a kind of transcendental rhythm, perhaps created by his proximity to death.

When I last spoke with him, he was in great spirits, in spite of his body's daily betrayals, and he said two things that shed light on this final book. Speaking about our shared working-class backgrounds, he mentioned that his nearness to death made him ask two questions. First: "What happens to a tough guy when his arms and legs don't work and he has a stomach full of liquids?" Second, "If I'm going to die in three or four weeks, shall I buy a new shirt?" Both of these questions suggest the ongoing dialectic of Marcus' poetry, since poetry, unlike us poets, never dies. In these final poems, Mort asks: how does one maintain one's sense of humor and write porms when faced with the big questions, which even death pales before.

If Mort was underappreciated before, I would suggest it was because he never really shared the fashionable cynicism of our times. He certainly bore witness to life's ironies and paradoxes, and he was a master at creating that "dark uncomfortable metaphor" Russell Edson has spoken of. But Mort was always hopeful, even optimistic. He would not give up on literature or life, even if the latter was giving up on him. The second poem in a *The Dark Figure in the Doorway,* called "Prayer," reads as follows:

There is a story in an upraised head,
an averted eye, a wavering smile;
in an angry shout and rolling laughter.

There is a story in a rusty coat hanger,
a discarded shoe, a faded tapestry;
in a broken cup, a wedding ring.

There is a story in a wolf, a cow, a bee,
flowering honeysuckle, a brittle weed;
in a rock, a pebble, a grain of sand.

Whoever or whatever you are
that resides in the center of the universe
with lightning, static and whirling dust,

permit me to retell these stories
without meanness of spirit
or self-serving words.

Here is Mort in a nutshell. All of his verse and prose poetry has always been about telling stories to make sense of the world. No matter how parabolic his poems, and Mort is one of our great fabulatists, his narratives have always been rooted in details, like the ones mentioned above. In "Prayer" Mort's humility also shines through, as he asks us to listen to him while promising not to be mean-spirited or egotistical, for Mort has always had a contempt for the ego and how it destroys authentic poetry. *In The Dark Figure in the Doorway* he seems more interested in us than himself or his deteriorating physical condition. This unselfishness accounts for the many times he directly addresses the reader as "you." It's as if he's saying, "Time is running out. Pay attention." "The secret / is, simply, / that I am / a teller / of secrets," and he wants to share them with us.

In his brilliant title poem, "The Dark Figure in the Doorway," referring to the man standing in the background of Velasquez's famous painting, *Las Meninas,* Mort writes that this dark figure is the "one who imbues / a work of art /with meaning / beyond itself. / Even the painter [substitute poet] / and his clever ruse / are less important than this messenger."

In The Dark Figure in the Doorway, I think we readers are the dark figure, giving life to the poet's final words as another dark figure hovers in the threshold, waiting to usher the poet into a different world. We must pay attention to Mort's stories and metaphors, even if he himself often becomes frustrated because his words sometimes fail. "At times I want to curse my words," he writes:

> because no one, it seems, wants to hear them;
> because they're breath that will rise, invisible,
> and coil flat and away, unseen by anyone,
> unlike smoke that flows upwards, thrashes
> in wind, is splintered by rain, before it too
> disappears. But there seems to be no escape,
> since curses, whether they're muttered
> or written, are words as well as emotions.

But this exasperation fades towards the end of the poem when he writes what resembles a personal manifesto but one all of us poets can live by:

> At times I want to curse my words
> because I know they will change nothing,
> but I never do—no, never, because the words
> are all I have and I must wait patiently
> for a message from another city,
> from a country beyond the sea,
> or even from the next street, knowing
> other words are not likely to arrive
> but I must continue using mine anyway.

Throughout *The Dark Figure in the Doorway* the "other words" do arrive to create poems that effortlessly connect with each other: poems about writing, about writers, about empty nuclear silos in Nebraska, and about memories from the poet's life. There are short poems, long poems, and also prose poems. Yet never does this multifariousness dissolve into incoherency, partly because by now Mort has the achieved improvisational dexterity of a jazz master, a comparison he would've appreciated.

But I think there is even more at work here. There is a structural principle organic to poetry itself, one Mort seems to recognize in his prose poem called, appropriately, "The Poem."

> A poem should speak not only to the head and heart but to the reader's cells, where the seeds of the universe's purpose have been embedded since the beginning of time, as if our chromosomes have been laid down like paving stones, one after another, and provide a silent, sure direction for us beyond rational understanding. The successful poem, then, taps each cell with an instinctive kind of knowing that causes it to resonate like a gong, until the millions of cells in the reader's body for an instant become an orchestra that trembles and swells with the music of recognition, a symphony of cosmic plenitude and unity.

What better description of the way *The Dark Figure in the Doorway* works thematically and stylistically, how it begins with the personal, then slowly and deliberately morphs into the universal, leaving us with that orchestral sensation that, as he writes, "trembles and swells with the music of recognition, a symphony of cosmic plenitude and unity." Mort is certainly the right conductor for this kind of symphony, and by the end of *The Dark Figure in the Doorway*, we feel privileged to have participated in his final composition.

Thanks, Mort.

for all those I've loved
and all those I haven't

"Our words are the children of many people
They are sown, are born like infants,
take rooot, are nourished with blood.
As pine trees
hold the wind's imprint
after the wind is gone, is no longer there,
so words
retain a man's imprint
after the man is gone, no longer there."

"Three Secret Poems"
George Sefaris

I

THE EIGHTH DAY

THE FIRST LAUGH

The first laugh was God creating the universe. That guffaw is still exploding in all directions, hollowing out and filling the farthest reaches of space.

What could have been so funny? The idea of light and sound after all that darkness and silence? After the eons of brooding and grumbling?

It must have been something bigger than we can imagine, something that elicited more than a cackle, a chortle, a chuckle or giggle, a snicker or titter.

Something, say, as big as a billion chandeliers of stars, millions of spinning galaxies with super nova popping like flashbulbs in their midst.

Or maybe not. Maybe something as small as an ocean or a mountain, a whale or an elephant, or even us.

PRAYER

There is a story in an upraised head,
an averted eye, a wavering smile;
in an angry shout and rolling laughter.

There is a story in a rusty coat hanger,
a discarded shoe, a faded tapestry;
in a broken cup, a wedding ring.

There is a story in a wolf, a cow, a bee,
a flowering honeysuckle, a brittle weed;
in a rock, a pebble, a grain of sand.

Whoever or whatever You are
that resides in the center of the universe
with lightning, static and whirling dust,

permit me to retell these stories
without meanness of spirit
or self-serving words.

THE SECRET

Come closer.
I'm going
to tell you
a secret.
The secret
is, simply,
that I am
a teller
of secrets.
But, of course,
you knew that.
It is the
reason why
you bend close
to this page—
to hear what
no one else
has told you.
Not that you
are concerned
with my life,
but if you
can find out
what I've done
or dreamt of
maybe you
can explain
your actions
and dreamings
to yourself.
So come here,
lean closer,

and listen:
I'm going
to tell you
a secret.

THAT'S WHAT YOU WRITE ABOUT

When you hear
the beak scratch
of birdsong
as your pen
noses through
the rustling
leaves of lined
white paper,
think of the tree
the paper
once was: all
those forests
whose voices
are trapped now
in the hard
winds beneath
the buried
skies of coal.

The sound of
those voices,
or just the
memory
of those trees
and forests—
that's what you
write about.

THE MEASURE, THE BREATH

Lorca, 1936. They stood him against the wall
of his thirty-eight years. He measured up well.

But the measure changes. What breaths we draw
are mossy buckets bumping foot by foot
from the lung's well and carved with faded initials.

And the line changes: the fixed foot unhobbled,
striding with a new pace, the breath struggling to keep up.

We learn to say over whatever needs to be said,
yes, "getting the words right," but more
the length it takes to breathe the phrase,
the sentence—the lengths to which we'll go:
breaths longer or tighter, of more duration or less,
the measure swinging like a fist from the lungs
that drove it to the ears that hear.

Generations of cells
tremble beyond words, small winds the ears can't hear:
vibrations of grandfathers teaching the old language,
the laws, the measures we should take.

But the measure is ours, the accumulation, a city dump,
the sound a new duration of breath saying the old words
with renewed force, the dead getting their weight behind it,
exerting pressures we will never understand.

One way or another, there is always the struggle for breath,
the placing of one foot before the other,
as we trudge through the city. Measure of the voice.
Of each person. Of every breath we take.

A POEM

He was a professor of Philology, named Richard, a fellow countryman. We had met on the bus from Nauplia to Epidaurus, and had started talking, and were now strolling through the countryside toward the famous theater. He wore jeans and a faded blue work shirt, and every once in a while the sunlight flashed off his steel-rimmed glasses, as we talked about Greek poetry and culture.

We were so intent on our conversation that it was almost a surprise to find ourselves suddenly standing above the open-air amphitheater where the Greeks had intoned the sacred words of human passions and loss for more than 2000 years. We were silent for a few moments, looking down at the empty stone benches that had once seated twelve thousand people, when Richard, almost whispering to himself, said in a monotone:

"A poem should speak not only to the head and heart but to the reader's cells, where the seeds of the universe's purpose have been embedded since the beginning of time, as if our chromosomes have been laid down like paving stones, one after another, and provide a silent, sure direction for us beyond rational understanding. The successful poem, then, taps each cell with an instinctive kind of knowing that causes it to resonate like a gong, until the millions of cells in the reader's body for an instant become an orchestra that trembles and swells with the music of recognition, a symphony of cosmic plenitude and unity."

Nothing more. He picked up a stone and tossed it into the pine trees that surrounded the theater, then walked off, kicking up puffs of dust as he went.

AT 31

At 31, I entered Miguel Hernandez last year,
having outlived Keats by five, Shelley by one.
Rimbaud, six years ahead in Africa, watched
his right leg swell like a giant asparagus;
and Crane, his drowned eyes full of fathers,
dragged chains of seaweed only two years away.

That night, my brothers, when I was almost asleep,
I heard you call from the road, throwing
your words like stones at my window.
But when I came to the sill and looked out,
you didn't ask me to follow, just stood mute:
hands open, heads upraised in the moonlight,
as though waiting for something I was expected to say.

LIVING WITH SU DONG-PO

for Deng Ming-Dao

For years I've served him,
the houseboy who snored
like thunder and didn't wake
when, drunk, he banged
on the gate with his staff
to let him in; the boy he leaned
against tipsily as he stood
on East Slope, watching
the moonlit river far below
and the little boat unmoored
and drifting into the distance.
"Master," I said, "you'll catch
your death." He didn't move,
just stood and watched,
and I watched with him.
I held the reins of his horse
when he dismounted that day
in the snow-tumbled village
where everyone was dead
or gone. He was surprised
because the first snow
had fallen like blossoms
on the other side of the ridge.
I remember his expression:
it was as much incomprehension
as sorrow, the same expression
that creased his features
eight years later, when he realized
he hadn't the inner strength

to free the convicts
as a New Year's gift.

I'm 67 now,
but he hasn't aged a day.
I squat in a corner of the room,
waiting as he sits at the table
beside the lantern, leaving
in the wake of his brush
fins and flukes, shiny and black,
an orderly school of glossy backs
swooping across the page. "More ink!"
he'll say, or "Tea!" but mostly,
"Wine, boy: where's the wine?"
When I placed the wine jar
near the lamp the other night,
I thought I saw the little boat
among the dolphins and dragons,
adrift among whirlpools
and lashing tails. I said nothing;
I never do. It is enough to be there,
to have him every now and then
hand me the reins or lean
against me high above the river,
both of us silent, watching
the water swirl and eddy
as it slides to the sea.

HIS FIRST BODY

In his early boyhood, Luigi Pirandello had his first experience with death. The event would haunt his imagination and work for the rest of his life. He never wrote about the experience.

It is Summer, 1877,
in the Sicilian countryside.
The ten-year-old boy
had heard the adults
talk the day before
about the Frenchman
who had killed himself
and about the unclaimed body
that because of the heat
had been taken to the cellar
of the abandoned tower
just north of town.
During the siesta
the following day,
while the grown-ups slept,
the boy crept from the house
into the searing sun.
Had the Frenchman
used a knife to his throat,
a pistol to his head, a rope
thrown over a beam?
Would the boy be able to look?
Did he really want to find out?

The town and the road
and the overgrown path

were empty, the door
to the cellar not only
unlocked but partly open.
He entered the darkness
with its odors of vinegar,
old wine barrels, manure
and straw. And there
on a table under a sheet,
like a statue not waiting
to be unveiled but almost,
it seemed to the boy,
waiting for the command
to come back to life,
was the undefined thing
he had come to see,
had wondered about
all night and morning,
and now approached
with stuttering steps,
horrified at its hidden shape.
But just as he reached out
a hand—was it his own,
trembling there so far away
at the end of his arm?—
he heard a scuffling
somewhere in the gloom
against a farther wall.

He tried to turn, to run,
but the shoes encasing his feet
were clamped to the floor,
and he stood, unable to move,

as rigid as the figure
under the sheet.
He strained to see whatever
was scuttling about
in the dimly lit straw,
and eventually he could detect,
thrashing in the shadows,
a man and woman,
her legs thrown high
and the man, between them,
thrusting and grunting.
The woman moaned,
but in a way the boy
had never heard before,
not a whimpering, no,
nor a stifled wail,
but a crooning at first,
a sound that rose
to a singing pitch
so pure and high
it was more frightening
than the figure
beneath the sheet,
and the boy turned
and with a strangled cry
ran from the cellar
into the sudden light
where the distant houses,
he now understood,
enclosed not only people
but secrets forever
beyond his sight.

THIS TERRIBLE COLD

I have a terrible cold
And everyone knows how terrible colds
Change the whole structure of the universe . . .

—Fernando Pessoa

Thank you, Fernando Pessoa, not for this terrible cold
but for confirming what I've long suspected,
that terrible colds alter the structure of the universe,
that those orbits, tracks, and planetary paths,
those cycles of intergalactic release and contraction,
those tides of spiritual expansion and regression
which splash like smoke through the cosmos,
can cause metaphysics to breathe its last
in a single universal sneeze.

I have lost a whole day, maybe two or three,
from among the orbits, tracks, planetary paths, etc.,
lost a day from looking into alleys and along boulevards
for those moments of heightened consciousness
that make each day a many-sided poem,
and all because the muse won't make a house call
to this stuffed head upon a platter,
to this lisper of lost dreams with his plugged-up nose.

AT TIMES I WANT TO CURSE MY WORDS

At times I want to curse my words
because no one, it seems, wants to hear them;
because they're breath that will rise, invisible,
and coil flat and away, unseen by anyone,
unlike smoke that flows upwards, thrashes
in wind, is splintered by rain, before it too
disappears. But there seems to be no escape,
since curses, whether they're muttered
or written, are words as well as emotions.

At times I want to curse my words
because whether I chant them, sing them,
intone them with reverence or anger,
I can't lay them on a table and dissect them,
studying their heartbeats to learn
their meanings or why I said them
or what I hoped they would bring me,
as if they were homing pigeons
who would return from another city
or a country beyond the sea
with fresh messages strapped to their legs
that would encourage and even enlighten me.

Is that what I expected, tending the coop
on my roof, that fragile structure
of chicken wire and rotten boards:
cleaning it out, leaving the hard seeds
and fresh newspapers on the floor,
always alert for the hawks that only I
and the other pigeon keepers know
sail over the city, endlessly hunting?

At times I want to curse my words
because I know they will change nothing,
but I never do—no, never, because the words
are all I have and I must wait patiently
for a message from another city,
from a country beyond the sea,
or even from the next street, knowing
other words are not likely to arrive
but I must continue using mine anyway,
uttering them with such precision,
charging them with such vibrancy
that they'll fly from my rooftop
in a dither of wings to god knows where
among the gliding hawks wheeling above
and the sirens wailing in the streets below.

THE EIGHTH DAY

We live in the eighth day
and the ones that follow, and the poets
attempt to sing the first seven days
into existence once again
for us to remember, to dream
our way back to.

But it's no use:
we live in the eighth day
and wade through all the rubbish
that's accumulated since then—
baby carriages, broken bottles,
toppled palace walls, spears,
rusty helmets, arrowheads.

What use
is it to remember? Can we,
really, bulldoze our way back
like the man on the machine
in the city dump, or like him
do we just bury the past to dig
it up and haul it to the next mound?

All the mounds and middens
that blister the Earth. All the bones
beneath hills. We are the generations
whose longings litter the planet
between the beginning
and the end.

Meanwhile,
we raise our children

like crops from the earth,
cannibalizing the past
to feed the future, and the poets,
sitting atop the bone pile,
continue to sing of what is gone

and what might have been.

RADIO

For 65 years I've waited to hear the words of God,
expecting them to resonate from the heavens
in a thunder clap over the planet—orations
of approval or bellows of anger, like the words
of a grandfather speaking to the head of a child.

All that time I ignored or half-listened
to the radio that sits like a miniature cathedral
on the living-room table, and from whose depths,
muffled and staticky, come news reports
of traffic congestion and foreign invasions;

bulletins of airline crashes on snowy mountainsides,
strikes at factories, sales at department stores,
someone kicking a goal at the last second of play,
dance band music, shrieks of electrocuted guitars,
terrorists bombing and toothpastes brightening.

These alternate with announcements
of mastodons encased as if alive in blocks of ice,
geese departing into sunsets and oceans arriving
like giggling girls tumbling their bodies
into the arms of their lovers; hurricanes, famines;

politicians announcing their candidacy one day
and declaring their take-over of the country the next;
the announcer at Lakehurst in 1937, crying out,
as he watches the mooring zeppelin explode into flame,
"Oh, the humanity!" —or is it "The Horror! The Horror!"

Now we beam radio signals into deep space,
scanning the heavens in our solitary vigil for words

that will redeem us. But maybe there is no redemption, and day after day God is proclaiming the way of his world from the miniature cathedral in the living-room.

GIVE & TAKE

"You've got to take more than you give,"
says Johnny Longo in a taxi going to the fights.

He's got three bets on a Puerto Rican lightweight
who lays down in the third.

When we taxi back uptown, he rips up the program.
"Life's a bitch," he says. I nod, and watch the streets

sliding backwards. "Know what's wrong with you?"
he says. "You think too much."

"You've got to give more than you take," I say.
"Yeah," he says, "that's what I mean."

FORGIVENESS

I.

I heard the man
before I saw him.
He was kneeling
in an alley
off Broadway
and 45th street
one summer night,
rocking back and
forth, muttering,
"Forgive me!
Forgive me!"
At first, I thought
he was bending
over a dog, then
I thought, no, his grief
is too great: it
must be a child,
and I hurried to help.
There was no dog,
no child. The man
was bending
over his shadow,
pleading with it,
"Forgive me!
Forgive me!"

2.

She was my mother's friend,
small and wistful.

Her husband had been gassed
at Auschwitz

and the numbers branded
on her forearm

were clearly visible.
It was years

before I could ask her
about them.

She smiled and touched my face.
"They are a sign,"

she said, "that I have been
forgiven."

SUMMER, 1953

Summer, 1953. If I can mop the lobby,
clean the furnace, and roll the ash cans full of cinders
to the street by 11:30, I can get off early. The pattern
was always the same: rushed to the late night deli
on 50th for a turkey on rye with Russian dressing,
munched on it as I strode to 52nd Street, then west
eight blocks to Broadway and Birdland, paying
the cover charge and flashing my false ID.
Downstairs it was shadows and cool music.
I'd sit at the bar, buy the musicians drinks
on their breaks: Stan Getz, Sonny Stitt,
others I've forgotten; several times, the Pres,
Lester Young, who nodded at all I said
and sipped his beer, staring at the mirror behind the bar,
thinking of music or misery, which by then
may have been the same; or I watched Billy Eckstine
in a duet try to feel up Sarah Vaughan,
who gave him a resounding slap that was a pure note,
in perfect pitch, and Eckstine smiled. Once,
sitting next to Miles Davis in his shades,
I offered to buy him a beer, and without turning
he replied with quiet finality those words
I've never forgotten, "Fuck off, kid."
Birdland, and Basin Street next door,
Roseland Ballroom down the street
with the driving rhythms and muted trumpets
of maybe Woody Herman's big band,
and the Palladium up the street,
where Perez Prado and Tito Puente
blared their brass mambos and cha-cha-chas,
until on those warm nights it seemed
the street was made of music, a glass crescendo,

a shower of sound that stippled the air
and prickled the skin. The Buddha says
accept the house being torn down:
house, no house: both are illusions.
The poet says, remember those warm nights
when music prickled your skin.

WHITE CASTLE, 1954

White Castle again: 3 a.m., Saturday,
across the street from the subway station
at Continental and 71st.
I approach the counter with the winos, frat boys, toughs,
and insomniac old men with nowhere to go:
my Saturday night routine, and theirs. Three months
and my balls just as achy as my bloodshot eyes,
as they have been the week before
and for the months before that, but I
nod to the others, take a stool at the counter,
and bury my woes in a cup of coffee
and three, maybe four burgers to start.
If there is a halfway house to heaven,
or at least to understanding, it is here,
watching the counter man slap the burgers,
thin as cheesecloth, on the grill, shake salt
and pepper on the raw side and dump
ice cream scoops of chopped onions
and pickle on top, flip them over with a sizzle,
and two minutes later shove them onto buns.
His skill and endless repetition
bring a clarity or at least a satisfaction
that here things are as they should be.
The aroma in this small, tight room
has become an all pervasive incense
that hours ago sweetened or soured
the regrets of everyone who sits here
with his own worries. Not a woman
in the place, not at this hour: a male way station
where we can figure out what our night
was all about. Outside, it's a glossy white castle:
turrets and crenellated roof, and I can imagine

that all of us are knights who have been sent forth
on labors none of us can understand.

WONDERING

Wondering what it's all about,
a spaniel tugs the oozing sheet.
I sit at the sill, staring out.

A cop sprints over with a shout,
clubbing the dog till it retreats.
Wondering what it's all about,

A child in bloomers, navel out,
jumps in the blood, slapping her feet.
I sit at the sill. Staring out

her window with a lipstick pout,
a woman yawns, her make-up neat,
wondering. What it's all about

Is that someone's dead, a stout
lump in the linen, a piece of meat.
I sit. At their sills, staring out,

the neighbors chat. Some frown in doubt,
stretch their arms, go in to eat.
Wondering what it's all about
I sit at the sill, staring out.

SILOS

I'd drive past them on sun-drenched afternoons
in Iowa and Nebraska, white concrete buildings
five and six storeys high, filled with grain
that could feed entire nations. And then
there were the other silos, also five and six storeys high,
that I couldn't see from the road but knew
were somewhere underground and housed the missiles
whose warheads were aimed, when their roofs slid away,
toward other countries.

The missiles are gone now,
but the silos are still there: empty tubes
of crumbling concrete and dangling wires, a reminder
of that presence just below our consciousness
that feeds our compulsions to kill and be killed.
Are these the responses that divide us now,
the same ones that surfaced in the caves of Cro-Magnon
and Neanderthal, where one fur-clad group
imagined spearheads in the flames of fire pits,
and the other painted caribou and bison
on the shadowy walls, both groups envisioning
an outside world where the ice was melting
and the valleys spread green and ready
for their different kinds of cultivation?

THE GOVERNOR'S SON

We did not lash ourselves in honor of the Governor's son, nor place our tongues on his parents' tender parts.

They approached us almost mincingly. They held out their hands. But we had suffered too much. We accepted their jewels with mutterings, remembering that the Provost had approached us in a similar fashion when he had taken our sons.

We were suddenly impatient with the Governor and his wife, with the breezes in their garments, with their young son who had arrived alone the night before.

The band played. The school children sang. The local dignitaries read their speeches.

The Governor stepped forward and expressed gratitude in reply. He said he was very tired but could recognize a loyal populace without knowing its name or speaking its dialect. He spoke of his son's arrival as a new beginning, a covenant with the future. He alluded to the elaborate embroidery on his wife's gown, remarking on the similarity between the garment's sumptuous plum-colored silk and the colors of the banners we had hung from our windows. He reminded us that anger was not love, and that trust was the scroll our grandfathers had signed and which, sealed in a golden pendant, he wore in the heavy chain around his neck. He said the house was strong only if it could withstand the fiercest storms; that the lion's eyes looked only for the weak on which to prey.

We were watching his son, who was staring at his father with as much pride as love. We remembered his expression the next day when we nailed the boy to the city gate. And that is why we chose the west gate, the one that overlooks the pit where the dogs were wrestling over his parents' limbs.

THE VILLAGE IS EMPTY

The village is empty,
the houses burnt out.
The only sound is the wind
moaning, a door banging.

In the dark wood,
there on the hill
above the buildings,
the trees shudder.

It is the same
night after night
when I return
to face this scene,

not only wondering
what happened here
but trying to discover
why everyone is gone.

I am not mourning
the dead but searching
for some sign of those
who were led away.

This is not my village,
or even my country.
It is the village
we heard about

on the news report
yesterday and today

and will hear about
tomorrow and the day

after that, the one where
all of us were rounded up
and led away yesterday,
today, and tomorrow.

THE MAN WITH THE MOUSTACHE

The man with the moustache is heavyset and browned,
tanned by days of sitting with his companions on the wharf,
joking, smoking, and drinking beer on the shores
of this Balkan village on the Adriatic Sea. "Pivo, pivo," he calls,
and his admirers scoot to get him can after can of beer
from a nearby store. Scars on his arms and cheeks,
calloused, grasping hands—he's a rough one in a rough crowd,
and the first day my wife and I appear, our eyes lock
as we size each other up—middle-aged men
from different countries, if not from different worlds.
Then, having seen enough, his gaze slides to my wife.
Oblivious, she spreads her towel and settles recumbent
and sighing in the sun. He mutters something to his friends,
who laugh, then turns to me and lifts his chin, jaws tight,
and glares. My jaws tighten too, and I glare back.

The muttering, the laughter, the stares—for four days
it's the same. Even today, the ritual is repeated,
but more as a formality, a weary greeting between men
who recognize each other in passing but do not share
language, customs or any common thing.
The hours pass in the hot, sun-drenched afternoon.
The man and his friends drink, swim, shout and laugh.
He dog-paddles, dives, splashes and swoops, and an hour ago
rose to the surface with an object in his hand
that he placed gently on the pier—a black spiny creature
big as his palm. The man remained in the water,
only his head and shoulders showing above the wharf,
as his hands caged the spiny thing, coaxed it this way and that
or nudged it forward with a finger to make it move.
For all that prodding, the animal remained inert.
But the man never grew impatient, and his examination

was so intense that every so often, as if coming up for air,
he would dart an almost embarrassed glance around the pier,
or toward his preoccupied companions who roughhoused
on the landing twenty yards away. Then he would return
to his find, turning it over and pressing it gently,
all the while bending his head close to the quills
like a watchmaker studying the interior of a clock.

He was so absorbed, he never noticed me watching him
from beneath a tree, as his thick fingers first
became a cradle, then pushed the creature forward
as if it were an infant he was teaching how to walk.
The man's jaw went slack as his absorption rose
and he became oblivious to everything around him.
Once he rinsed the animal below the pier.
Next he lifted it to the slab again and caressed
the spines and belly. But no matter what he did,
the creature lay there and wouldn't move.
Finally, as if releasing a bottle with a message inside,
the man lifted it again, turned, and offered it to the sea,
watching it for several minutes as, I guess,
it got its watery bearings and crawled away.
The man shivered, shook himself free, looked up,
and caught my gaze. His chin hardened. He glared.
Then, suddenly, he relaxed and nodded. I nodded back.

OUR NEIGHBOR IN THE MOUNTAINS

Our neighbor in the mountains
apologizes for the noise he made last night,
when, with arms raised, he hooted, "Shoo! Shoo!"
He says he was at his window, shooing away a bear
who had gotten into the garbage. "Unlatched
the shed where the cans are kept
and carried one away. He was this big,"
he says, spreading his arms wide overhead.

My wife and I heard nothing, slept through it all,
and, like good neighbors, now stand in the sunlight
by the garage door, listening politely.
He's not apologizing, really. Doesn't care
if we think he's a drunk or a wife beater.
It's his excitement he wants to communicate,
that moment, "at exactly 12:30 a.m.,"
when the commotion brought him to the window
to see the shaggy shape rummaging through the rubbish,
and he had shouted, and the bear had turned
and rose to a height the man would never have imagined,
before carrying the can to the driveway
where we stand now. "He dumped it here,
nosed around, and left. I cleaned it up.
Didn't want you to think, you know,
I came onto your property without permission,"
and his voice trails off.

                                        I nod that it's okay,
still the good neighbor, and think
that what led the man to cross the lawn
was his need to retrieve *his* property
of squashed soup cans, plastic cups and chicken bones,

and only the bear was not concerned
about whose property was whose. I shrug,
"No big deal," I say, "we're not the owners anyway.
It belongs to our in-laws, and we're—"
"We rented our place, too—for a week," he grins.
"We're from back east: Philadelphia."

He's relaxed now, meeting an outsider like himself.
"God, he was big. Ever see one?" he asks,
and when I nod, we stand there for a moment
in comradely silence, contemplating the memory
of things that were and things that might have been,
like two retired British generals in an old movie
who have withdrawn to the study after dinner,
the heads of lions, elephants and deer
mounted on the walls around them.

AT 63

for Du Fu

Egrets dart beaks into the river.
The shallows ripple over their legs
like time's transparent silk,
as winds rumble from the gorges
where the old poet in exile
wept for his children and his nation.
I have lived a comfortable life,
my only grief the heart's tumults
wrestling in my chest, and the fear
that the old poet's words would be my own.
Tonight I taste his poems in my mouth
and speak them into the new millennium.

NEW YEAR'S EVE

It's gotten so
I'm almost
ashamed
to write
a funny poem.
Even my wife
upbraids me.
In this day
and age things
are too final,
each event
is seasoned
with our doom,
like a roast
heading
inevitably
toward the oven.
Still, I can't
stop laughing:
all the terror,
tragedy,
injustice, wars,
all the hatreds,
and jealousies
that we first
experienced
in those caves
dripping
with shadows
and paint-
smeared walls—
are still around,

and it seems
that the only
sanity
is to laugh
insanely.
So understand
this poet,
or know that he'll
stop laughing
when the world
becomes,
as it's
becoming,
too funny
for words.

THE GODS ARE PLAYING TENNIS WITH OUR LIVES

The Gods are playing tennis with our lives,
swatting the balls in all directions
into the darkness out of play.

Do they know where each ball lands
after it's bounded off beyond their sight?
Is it just a game to them? Do they care?

The Earth tumbles through the heavens
as if it had ricocheted off the net
and into the forest beyond the court.

Where is it headed, blisters of gas
and bushes of fire erupting in the distance
and everywhere around it as it rolls?

The gods are playing tennis with our lives
and no one cares. Like mites on a berry,
we sun ourselves, stroll to the office,

scamper in hordes toward other hordes
that scamper toward us—frothing at the mouth,
yelling oaths, brandishing guns and spears.

We pray to our mite gods and kill
other mites who pray to theirs
while this ball we're on bounds off

to somewhere called the future,
a space we hurtle through
on our way to somewhere else,

and that somewhere is where we stop
and the ball shrivels to either a cinder
or a blister of gas that other balls roll past.

Do you worry if she loves you,
or if he's faithful, or who will own
the largest, most luxurious house?

Friends, what is it that you're listening for?
Do you hear the volleyings in deep space?
The Gods are playing tennis with our lives.

GOODBYE TO ALL THAT

I sit above the green Pacific
in a white house, reading Cassidy's letter.
"Bernie's gone," he writes.
Bernie gone now, his big hands
clamped like handcuffs around the basketball:
"*1* on *1* for a buck, two bucks, come on!"
Forty foot jumpers in the dark of Central Park
for rapists and muggers to marvel at:
"He hits," he'd shout with each shot,
"the little man with the fetching face
hits for a big deuce—another TA-WHO!"
Those hands cradling my shoulders,
like giant wrenches, hooked, in the end,
around the urinous air
in Bellevue's psycho ward. Bernie gone.
And Camello gone with hot grounds
and line drive doubles to left center:
"He's a fag, man, don't chu know?
He try to get me in the bushes once,
so I hit him with the bat. He no trouble
after that, and I'm the best catcher he ever have."
Camello gone to a taxi driver's paunch,
wife and three kids in the tenements
and stabbed for pocket change by a junkie fare.
And Cassidy gone, too: thin and red-haired,
skin like candle wax, teeth clenched and laughing,
as he hunched, dipped a shoulder,
flicked a jab, and drove a right
into my belly, elbows pumping
with piston body punches and counters to the head.
Cassidy gone to a mansion on Long Island,
expensive booze, racism, and a broker's firm:

"What this country needs is a good five-cent
shit-kicking Irish cop," he writes, "and mark my words
we're going to clean this country up."

THE BOY IN THE SANDBOX

Who is this boy staring at me with my eyes? What does he see? An old man looks back at him across the years, knowing what the boy does not know, having dreamt and hoped what the boy is too young to understand. I sift through the sand grains of my life and find what the boy does: play, not memories; repetition, not meaning. In an hour, the boy will go into a world of bitterness and worries, failures and divorces, deaths, wars and disappointments that will bring him to this photograph in his mother's drawer after her death, that woman whose eyes saw the city the boy grew up in from the deck of a cattle boat carrying her and her six-year-old eyes from a Europe he didn't know existed. What did she see, wish for, dream of, with those eyes the boy never thought to look into, any more than the old man did or the old man's daughters who turn away from him and a past that is longer than the boy, the old man, or his daughters can imagine?

THESE HANDS

I used to think my hands were wings.
I was young and I wanted to fly:
fly over the school and buildings on the street;
over the neighborhood and city;
over highways, mountains, small farms
surrounded by orderly furrowed fields;
over dirt roads, forests, and plains,
and those slim rivers—gold filaments
in the sunlight—that curved back and forth
into the distance. I wanted to fly into the night,
and maybe soar all the way to heaven,
or at least to the hidden valley in the Himalayas
where I knew there was something I wanted,
even if I couldn't explain what it was.
I sat at my desk and my hands waited.
They weren't wings. They were pets expecting
commands that never came. And that's
how it was for longer than I can remember.

Now when I wake each morning
my hands lift water from the faucet
and cradle my face. They hold me, cling
to my features, caress my nose and cheeks,
cover my eyes with a cool tenderness.
I can't remember the day I no longer needed flight,
when I first looked at my dripping face
in the mirror, and then inspected my palms
to see if the impression of my features was still there,
as if to verify that whoever I was the previous day
had traveled through the night and endured.
And I don't recall when I first saw my hands raise
the water like an offering I made to myself

and at the same time I bent to accept,
nor when I knew my hands were more than hands,
not wings nor pets, but two forgotten maps
whose roads run wild to the edge of an ancient sea.

II

THE DARK FIGURE IN THE DOORWAY

PAINTINGS

In museums and galleries, evenly spaced on the walls, windows open onto wheat fields in southern France, mountains and rivers in Ming Dynasty China, or sills where old women with tired faces in Amsterdam and young mothers with glowing infants in Verona sit and stare at us.

We look into rooms where Japanese courtesans, heads turned away, gaze at hand mirrors, or we peer into town squares where troops of men, pikes and helmets glinting in the firelight, swagger through the night.

We look through those windows, but never enter them. Never stare out at ourselves peering in, wanting to understand. Never allow ourselves to see that homeless person with questioning gaze, standing outside the living room window.

CHAGALL'S DAY

Music is lost old men scratching it from violins. They show up in beards and black boots wherever someone is talking or groups of people converse, at weddings and funerals. Small in black overcoats and short-billed caps, they arrive from far off, out of place with their violins and an awkwardness in how they stand.

Sun at their backs, they stoop through afternoons, bent by their knapsacks, by their violins, by the music. They appear from doorways, side streets, rooftops. The music is their being there, unscrolling through the marketplace.

The crowd bickers and bargains. Boys and girls lean like tongues from the windows, giggling and shouting, as the old men hobble around elbows and backs, accompanying the conversations, steering them into their music before wandering off to another village.

They move with the sun as it slips down the sky, and are gone at the tops of hills, their music scraping the edges of evening.

Night pours out of the earth. The market empties its people to houses and huts. Now, rising on the strains of half-remembered songs, lovers float through windows and glide among the stars.

PAVEL TCHELITCHEW'S "HIDE AND SEEK"

Tchelitchew was a true mystic. He understood
the interconnectedness of things
and knew the body's only disease
was being alive. In "Hide and Seek,"
the Tree of Life is our family tree
that hides the children while bearing
their heads like decaying fruit. Actually,
the tree is more a birth canal than a tree.
It propels the unborn infants, heads first,
through the trunk and launches them
from the branches. Those melon-yellow heads,
half-green and moldy blue, threaded
with vermillion membranes and nerves
like fishing line nibbled by moss —
the more you stare at them, the more
you see they are composed of spider webs
and dandelions, jellied nests and mildew,
until nothing is what it seemed to be
the moment before: everything is becoming
something else right before your eyes.
And those hydrocephalic heads (each instant
more fungoid, more moldy and lichen-encrusted)
have turned what's left of their astonished faces
toward the tree trunk and the girl whose back
is toward us. They stare at her as she faces the tree
in a determined stance, her arms outstretched
as if to embrace it as her long-lost father
or to demand from it an explanation.

TCHELITCHEW'S CONTRADITIONS

Tchelitchew was so frightened of mice
that when he saw one at headquarters
during the Russian Civil War,
he leaped onto a table spread with a map
two generals were studying.

His terror of crossing water, even rowing
a boat across a pond, was well known.
And yet in his art he peeled back the skin
to show men and women webbed in blood vessels,
the bawling babies of their psyches
pushing through their facial bones.

In his painting "Phenomena," those he loved
appear as freaks, with enormous penises
and three breasts, but all are shown, he said,
"always in the most beautifully decayed colors."

Still, he was a good friend, and cured Dali—
who was terrified of everything—of being afraid
to use the subway, when he accompanied him
into the depths of those shrieking catacombs
and—as he does with us standing transfixed
but bewildered before his paintings—left him there.

THE DARK FIGURE IN THE DOORWAY

Wearing a silken silver gown,
the little princess
is staring at us
from the foreground
of the painting.
As if on stage,
she is brightly lit,
surrounded by dwarfs,
ladies in waiting,
and a recumbent hound,
and resembles a doll
placed in the middle
of her entourage.
Behind her to her right,
near a large canvas
whose back is toward us,
the painter, Velazquez,
stands half in shadow,
palette in one hand,
brush in the other,
while behind her
to her left, a nun
leans toward a courtier,
about to speak. On
the rear wall: paintings,
large canvases, hang,
almost obscured
by darkness, and a mirror
reflects the presence
of the king and queen
who must be observing
the scene from the same place

we do, as if they (or we)
are an audience
at a formal family event.

But, no, the painter
is standing in
the wrong place
to paint the scene.
Do you see it now?
It's the king and queen
who are being painted,
and the princess
and her entourage
are the audience
watching mama
and papa pose
for Señor Velazquez,
a clever ploy
which confuses
subject and viewer,
since we are standing
in the very spot
the royal couple
occupy, and see
what they do,
not what the painter
possibly can—
a post-modern
bit of fun devised
centuries before
the modern age
will have begun.

That ruse, however,
is not the reason I return
to this 10 foot painting
time and again. No,
it's the doorway cut
into the rear wall,
beside the mirror.
Flooded with light,
it illuminates
a dark figure
standing on the stairs.
He is about to leave
or enter—it's not clear
which. He is half-turned,
looking back into the room
toward us, or rather
toward the king and queen,
and it seems important,
more important
than anything
in the picture, whether
he is departing
or arriving,
as if the painting's
meaning
hinges on this point.
I can't say why.
Maybe because everyone
depicted is so still,
every object in its place,
and the only tension
is whether he leaves

or enters from the world
beyond the painting.
He is the dark figure
in the doorway,
the one who imbues
a work of art
with meaning
beyond itself.
Even the painter
and his clever ruse
are less important
than this messenger,
this intermediary
who carries the scene
as witness between
two worlds, the one
created by the painter's
skill and imagination
and the other
what the viewer
takes of it
into his daily life.

The little princess
will marry
the Emperor of Austria
ten years later,
when she is fifteen,
and will die at twenty-two.
The king and queen
will leave a halfwit heir,
who will die soon after,

and with them all
the Spanish Golden Age
will sink into oblivion.
But like the figure
in the doorway,
we hesitate today,
caught between yesterday
and tomorrow, aware
as never before
that we stand with one foot
in the painting
and one foot out,
sure only of this moment
when we look into the room
where the king and queen
pose for the painter
who stands with his back
toward us,
as do the doll-like princess
and her entourage,
and at our backs
we hear the laughter
and curses on the street,
while scattered around us
like stars at night
or the sunlit dust motes
of our afternoons
are all those possibilities
of who we were
and could have been
and one day
might become.

III

ALL WE CAN DO

LADYBUG

Today a Zen nun
came visiting.
Actually, she
had lost her way
and wandered
into my yard,
carrying
on her back
a lacquered orange
begging bowl
large as a shield.

Had
she hauled that bowl
all the way
from Japan, on
a pilgrimage
neither she nor I
could understand?

I couldn't ask
her that. I asked
myself, and now
you. She and I
were in separate
worlds, surrounded
by carapaces
of ignorant
intentions.

I
lifted my pen
like a hobo's stick
and with this bundle
of words, set out
toward you, as lost
as she was.

It's
spring again. No,
it's that moment
when I'm reminded
and set out
to remind you
that we're on
a pilgrimage
neither our words
nor intentions
can comprehend.

ROCKS AND TREES

At dusk, the rocks, huddled in hoods, rise from their knees and scurry forward. Rocks lean toward the dark; it is their preference. All day kicked by hooves, crushed by wheels, they hold fields in place, anchor our shadows. Now they hurry off to their own lives.

Even the trees rise, like ballerinas in heavy coats, and stride on tiptoe to their lovers' homes, like the farmhouse in the valley where the little boy taps on the window as they pass.

BEFORE & AFTER

After our breathing stilled
and the slippery patina
cooled on our skins,
I imagined us
lying side by side
like two separate statues
imbedded in marble,
as if we were half formed,
never to emerge from rock.
It hadn't been that way
the moment before
when we were one, bucking
against each other, fighting
our separateness until it
finally gave up for a moment
and let us fall through
each other's entangled arms.
"What are you thinking?" I asked.
"Nothing" you replied.
What is it I wanted words to say
where words had no place,
where knowing was not knowing?
Like the vase by the open window
that fell in a sudden gust.
Remember? Two green parakeets
were painted on it
amid scrolling red vines.
We didn't hear it
until it shattered, that vase
we could not replace.

WHAT I WANTED FROM WOMEN

What I wanted from women
was the essence of who they were
behind the face, deep in the heart,
the person breathing from every cell.
"What are you thinking," I'd ask
immediately after our breath stilled
and our slippery bodies lay side by side.
I couldn't see their faces in the dark;
but in the light, their expressions
didn't match what their words said.
I'm not sure when I first realized
the body lying next to me was not
the shape of the other but my shape.
"What are you thinking," I heard
myself saying, and knew whatever
the answer, it would be my own.

3 POEMS THAT MAKE YOU BEAUTIFUL

1.

Something—your hands
rummaging for dishes beneath the foam
while the white enameled stove
outlines the slope of your butt
held captive in designer jeans.
Neither priestess nor statue,
you stoop over the sink
as the suds shift back and forth
like the belly of a grumpy old man
dreaming of seaside girls.
That moment, that something,
when you raise your arms
and lift, shiny from the foam,
the dazzling edge of a plate.

2.

There is a loveliness
that goes as it comes:
water shadows, for one,
or your smile, darling,
which I'm never sure of.

"Sure!" you say,
and stride from the room
most sullenly.
That, too, goes as it comes
and sets a loveliness in you
more subtle than water shadows
but as continual.

3.

All over the apartment,
bits of you remain
when you are gone—
the wilted strands,
the looping pencil-lines of hair:
on desk, bathtub, dresser drawer—
why, I even find them
tangled in my crotch,
as if you hid them everywhere,
in all the rooms,
so that your presence
would be with me
when I bathed, ate,
or wrote a poem.

THE FARM WIFE'S DREAM

My nightdress keeps bouncing up, here in the dark.
Bracken and briar snatch at my ankles
and I whirl, shoulders twitching,
arms flung out, the soles of my slippers
barely touching the ground. Pulled over hills,
tugged along ridges, I'm the moon's puppet
guided by air. Small sounds the land makes
it makes under me, and others I'd almost forgotten:
the coughing of stones huddled in clover,
moist lips of growing that flutter and swell.
Flowers snap with the noise of small flags unfurling,
and weeds are all whispers with jaundiced breath.
I move in a running I hadn't known I'd begun,
back beyond valleys and moonlight,
past the shadow of the girl I once was
stirring bright water with an aimless finger,
past cows and creepers and battalions of corn,
past small farms flowing away on the hillsides,
until I come to the ferns near the bend in the river
and stop, finally, by the tree-darkened water
that extends like a long, possibly infinite breath.
Under a stone there's only the wet
and the gap where the stone's meant to be.
The insects are silent. The wind has collapsed.
Even the shadows are holding their breath.
I know this place, says a damp nest inside me.
It's here you began and now come to stay.
But this is a dream, a dream that I'm dancing:
I'm back in the house, in bed with my husband
who I've slept with for twenty years until now.
Why can't I wake? Why am I here by the river,
sitting on a flat rock, removing my slippers?

The eyes of small animals watch what I do,
and whirling inside, I stroll through the shallows
with slippers of water fitting my feet.
My body's too light to be me: two sons
and the weight of forty-five winters
have filled me with sand and the sharpest of winds.
Why have I come, and what was it sent me?
Should I sing in the dark and fill it with that?
Water hugging my hips—how long has it been?
I'd wear this river like a robe, hood for my head,
if I could sail out to sea and be lost in the fog.
But the small mouths of water suck at my skin,
rocks intercept my body's direction,
and I bump in a backwash padded with lilies
while the river continues beyond my breath.
Where am I going that I tremble and ache?
The water is speaking, but its words are slurred,
and voices inside me sob to sing out.
I'm floating inside—my skin is dark water
and my bones branch through me
with blossoms of blood. I'm here, here in the river.
In this dream of my life, my life has begun.

PEARS

The pears are all buttocks and hips. They lie on their sides, asleep in the blue bowl. Mothers at rest in a swimming pool of the gods, surrounded by sky.

Their heads are so small, without features. They could be anyone and therefore are no one, their slumber as anonymous as their faces.

Like those clay statuettes thousands of years old: the breasts, the wide hips, the tiny faces as blank as thumbs, the legs crumbled to sand eons ago.

The bright plaza painted blue in the sunlight. The one by the ruins of the Aztec temple. Did mothers once sleep behind shutters in the afternoon, dreaming of husbands and lovers who dreamt of them, dreaming of children who woke beyond their dreams as husbands and daughters?

The slope of my wife's hip as she sleeps, turned away from me. How many times have I reached for her and my hand come away with the afterbirth of a dream that vanished like phosphorescent foam?

The woman washed up on shore. No one could identify her. As her body lolled back and forth in the tide, no one could tell if she was arriving or departing.

MILY BALAKIREV (1837-1910): A LIFE IN MUSIC

1.

A fat little man with bulging eyes and pointed beard,
he would scamper into the street in only his shirtsleeves

and run after sleighs swishing through the snow,
shouting, "Cross yourselves! Make the sign! Repent!"

He was most concerned about the moral conduct of his dog,
and he would carry the animal clasped to his chest,
so it wouldn't be tempted by canines of the opposite sex.

If he found a flea, even a bedbug, in his apartment,
he would cup his hands, cage it in his palms
and gently place it on the windowsill.

2.

Tchaikovsky called him a "saintly prig"
because he was so self-righteous and tyrannical.

But as founder and leader of the *Russian 5*,
Balakirev may have had to play the general,

or at least the inspired military recruiter,
since he created the group from an army engineer,
"specializing in fortifications," a naval cadet,

a perfumed ensign in the Royal Guards,
an army doctor, and a chemist—exhorting them all
to sound the music slumbering in the Russian soul.

3.

He began composing before he understood
even the rudiments of composition.

No one in the group, in fact, knew anything
about the rules of music. All were self-taught,

and espoused "spontaneity" and "truth in music,"
guided by their probings of the Russian soul.
"Amateurs!" cried Tchaikovsky. "Gifted dilettantes!"

But Balakirev continued on, encouraging
his pupils to analyze their own and others' works
and to selflessly complete each other's scores.

4.

To Rimsky-Korsakov, he said, "I expect great things from you,
as an aged aunt does from her lawyer nephew."

He dismissed Mussorgsky for having "weak brains,"
but he is the one whose music has been forgotten.

Angry at Borodin for an imagined slight,
he was so overjoyed at hearing the composer
was working on a large orchestral score

that with moist eyes he took his protege's nose
between his second and third fingers and, standing
on his toes, gave him a resounding kiss.

5.

Borodin said of him: "He is so despotic;
he demands complete subordination to his wishes.

His nature is such that he requires
children he can fuss around like a nurse."

In 1872, he left the group, renouncing music
for a job as a clerk in a railroad station.
Two years later he returned, but never again to the 5.

By the time he died in 1910, forgotten and alone,
he had outlived all his early proteges, except Cui
who had stopped composing years before.

SNAPSHOT: JOHN WALTHER PLAYS THE CELLO

Christ, taken from the cross,
is in the arms of his beloved John
who revives from him
a moan of sorrow for all our sufferings.

LISTENING TO LOU HARRISON'S "SUITE FOR VIOLIN & AMERICAN GAMELAN" SHORTLY AFTER THE COMPOSER'S DEATH

As I listen to Lou Harrison's
"Suite for Violin and American Gamelan,"
a blue jay in the oak tree outside the window
shrieks and shrieks, louder and louder,
the same exclamation over and over again:
"I wrote that! I wrote that! I wrote that!"

SERENADE TO A CHRISTMAS TREE

Who would have thought
that I'd feel sorry
for the tree? As a child
I never had one,
but remember,
in others' homes,
how each one stood—
bejeweled
and all ashimmer
like a gypsy woman
gaudy with bracelets,
ribbons, and perfume
who waited in
a Russian night
for her lover's troika
to take her in.

Now, at thirty-two,
for my wife who's had them
and both our daughters,
I've bought this tree,
heady with pine tar
and shaking boughs
and the odor of shadows
on private hills,
and propped it
in the living room
where its aroma
has reminded me
of how it's dying
to decorate
my winter home.

I could have bought
aluminum,
a metal tree;
hung red baubles
on its clicking boughs,
and never cared
about fire, or needles,
or the odors of the hill.
But I wanted hills,
the long odors,
the possibility
of imbecilic flames:
I wanted
something that's alive
to share this room.

I guess I've made
my choice, then.
It comes down to this:
in choosing your death,
I choose my life.
It can't explain.
I only know
that old men are sleeping
in your wood, ungrained,
undone. Old woman,
you have waited long,
expectantly,
as we wait now
seated before you,

a little nervous
that you give to us
only what
we give to you—
tinsel, ribbons,
the vaguest of perfumes.
This poem, then,
is for your patience
and the rings that widen
into generations
where your death is
and where, finally,
we all belong.

THE BALLAD OF CASTLE ROCK, GUALALA, CALIFORNIA

My daughters, the castle
is anchored in the ocean
named Pacific which heaves
like a green armada
of whales spuming
sideways into the wind.
Twin towers (mudstone,
layers of hardened silt)
never open their windows
but enclose in their halls
a dwarf with bells
on his boots. He
swaggers into the room
of a princess asleep
on her canopied bed
with flames in her hair
and music asleep
in her eyes, a sight
which sends him
into a jabbing jig
of savage joy.
But so quiet is it
in those passageways
that even the dust
doesn't hear him
and continues to dream,
despite the thunk of his heels
and the silent lolloping
of the bells.

You'd
never know all this
to look at the rock,
its towers shrinking
under the knives
of the wind and the swords
of the sea. The galleries
have already been shorn
where the king and queen
once entertained
courtiers arriving
in giant shells
and ten thousand candles
lighted the windows
now boarded with mud
and barnacle rot.

My daughters,
it is an old story
I am repeating,
except that the princess
won't wake as the wife
of a wandering prince,
nor will the castle
be magically
whole again, swaying
with lights and music
and stewards hurrying
and courtiers laughing
and sauntering
through the halls.
This is the domain
of the dwarf, who roams

through the damp
and darkening halls
with dirty red beard,
tickling the bells
on his scuffed brown boots
into continuing silence
as he jigs from room to room.
And the music that sleeps
in the eyes of the princess
will never be heard,
no, never be heard,
unless you hear it,
my children, listening
to the ocean and the wind
singing against the rock
the townspeople,
out of wisdom or despair,
have named a castle.

THE WHIRLING DERVISH

I

He whirls because the winds
coax him to whirl whirling his robes.
It is easy to move with the wind
when the mind shifts in empty urns.
It is easy to shift as the mind shifts
when the journey has come to this,
blue sky and the white backs of sand.
Better to be a wind nosing the rims
of battered urns than a man in a desert.
Yet deserts are made by men,
not from the landscape
but the landscape's lack.
He whirls in the claws of the wind,
letting the dance explain him.
Breezes scurry like eager servants
and usher him into the dunes.

II

In the desert a hut may be a hill;
a pond, a wind-pawed level of sand:
his mind reciting old images
scoured from deep-hipped urns
remembers the ritual words.
He moves to them, in the old rhythm.
But the words are folded in the wind
and his comfort in them is gone.
Tufts of wind snatch at his heels.
His elbows swing out, filling his robes,

arms forming handles. He dances an urn,
and his mind, inventing new words,
constructs it. His sandals pause
as he tastes, then speaks the word.
The winds shift in another direction.

MY ANDALUSIA

These are the evenings
when the men in knickers
stroll with saffron kerchiefs
knotted behind their heads
and vermillion garters
like bouquets below their knees.
Drinking from bottles
or fingering flat guitars,
they appear at corners
in groups of three or four,
already talking too loudly,
their embroidered vests
unfastened like casual breaths.

They will walk all night,
fitting their women
into the shapes of their speech
and sipping the flavors
that float between their teeth.
They pass drunken friends,
boisterous nephews
with shirt fronts undone
who swagger to dances,
apprentices with faces of shadow
stumbling toward rented rooms,
and girls in butterfly dresses
who sit patiently on porches.

And always the women wonder
where they are going,
these men, these drunkards,
as they clear away dishes

and their young sons sleep
with heroines like bent trees
inside their dreams.
The streets are infinite,
circling like a black blood.
The town is as large as the night
or the inside of your head.
And if this never happened,
Compadre, it just did.

A DAY IN THE LIFE

l. Evening

Evening arrives
like departures
at a train station:
the shouts and kisses,
the hurried goodbyes,
and then the silence,
always the silence
on the empty platforms,
where only the children
and the women in black
remain, wavering shadows
in the failing light.

2. Night

Night is a cathedral
arching over the town:
the stars are chips of silver
embedded in the ceiling,
and the moon hangs,
a medallion suspended
from heavy black chains.
Its light silvers the roads
and swirls the ocean swells
beyond the tiny harbor
into pewter platters and bolts
of platinum-colored silk.
Like miniature game pieces,

the people on the streets
are hushed and look up,
refusing to move, knowing
this moment cannot last.

3. Waking

A muffled shout.
and then the white horse
vaulting through the window
and standing steaming
and trembling by the bed,
staring into the sunlight,
stomping, shaking its head.

4. The Return

My hands let go of the sky
and I float down into my body.
My feet and the floorboards
are strangers once again,
but they hold on to one another
like lovers who have been apart
for longer than they can remember.

5. Breakfast

This trembling coffee in the cup
is like the ideas inside my forehead:
shifting, uncertain in the wavering light.
I want more light on my thoughts,
I want to discover once and for all
what I can know and not know.
Only then will I be able to grasp
what the eyes see looking inward.

6. Noon

In the daydream I am lost in a field of wheat,
miles of wheat stretching to the horizon.
The stalks rustle higher than my head,
shaking and hissing like a golden fire,
but not a fire, what was once a fire —
dry stalks of flame, as if the field
is the surface of the sun after its death.
Then I am high above the field and see
that it is nothing more than a sunflower
and I strain to find myself crawling alone
among the roots of its blackened seeds.

7. Afternoon

There is not much difference
between feet and dry leaves.
Both flutter over the ground
and curl at the edges, finally
coming to rest in the earth.
But once the leaves were fingers.
They touched sunlight and wind
and raindrops ran down their palms.
The feet were always the same:
face down in the mud, staring
at stones and floorboards,
familiar with dust, cobwebs and dirt,
and only when their owners
would dance or dive into ponds
or otherwise kick up their heels
would they glimpse the sunlight
and smell the wind, recognizing
only the clouds that spend their days
trudging across the sky.

8. Shadow

I am no one,
less than
the shadow
at my side.
Going home
from work,
you see it
as you pass me
on the street.
But it is nothing
more than
a momentary
covering
on the sidewalk,
a cloud, a footfall,
a fragrance
that reminds you
of something
you can't quite
remember.

WHAT HAVE YOU THOUGHT ABOUT TODAY?

What have you thought about today?
You must ask yourself that question
at least once each time the Earth, your planet,
rotates on its axis as it whirls around the sun.
That is, what have you thought about
in the last 24 hours, in the last 1,440 minutes,
in the last 86,400 seconds?

If you sleep eight hours every night
that leaves you 16 hours, or 960 minutes,
or 57,600 seconds to think about something.

I believe that if you think about something
every 24 hours, if you think about it
with your liver, your lungs, your large
and small intestines—if you think about it
with your whole being—then you will not lose hope.

I'm not talking about just any thought,
like whether you've left the stove on
or if you took the one white and two red pills,
but something that will make your heart
lurch for a moment like the engine of a car
that for thirty years has been wearing
a shroud of cobwebs in the garage—something
that will make your mind start clicking
like the clock on the living-room mantle
that hasn't worked in a decade or two.

So, what have you thought about today?
What realization of universal sorrow
has so weighted your eyes that your tears
have fallen like bodies buried at sea
on a moonless night off a foreign coast?
What thought caused a smile to stretch on your lips
as if it had just woken from a long sleep—
the same kind of smile that was on the lips
of the princess after the kiss woke her:
you know, the smile that began just before
she opened her eyes to behold,
wonder of wonders, the whole world,
brimming with its 24 hours, smiling at her.

SHADOWS

The shadows are thieves among the trees.
They creep from bush to bush, slip
from tree to tree, mingling with the leaves,
continually seeking a place to hide and observe.
I know what they're after, even here
in my backyard on a sunny day in spring.
In France, Croatia, Greece, I've seen them
watching and waiting. It's silly to always
be on guard like this. They're doing what they must
in what the wisest of us call "the scheme of things,"
and which, let me assure you, I accept.
Why worry then? Let them have the house
and all that's in it—in the drawers
and cupboards and secret places: let them have
the notes and scribbles and half-done poems,
valuable only to me but which they'll steal
on principle and toss into a field within a day.

Even in the house, I have observed the shadows
behind the paintings and photographs I hold dear—
the icon of St. Seraphim, the drawing of Lao Tzu
riding for eternity on the buffalo's back,
the etching of the ferocious bear, and the photo
of the Greek lauto player in the village crowd,
who swoons in ecstasy from the music
he's released into the air. All celebrate
the holiness and wonder of life, but the shadows
hide behind them, or slither from one to another
as if the objects were blank walls, there to provide
convenient cover and nothing more. It's gotten so
I spend my days observing shadows observing me,
although at times now I imagine a shadow at my back

and a hand settling on my shoulder, weightless,
reassuring, and I murmur, "This great life!
How lucky I've been!" and I turn and let it go.

THE SNOW OUTSIDE

The snow lies down
in the dark woods.
It is weary and emits
a soundless sigh.

It settles under the trees,
the hair of old men,
silent, still, fallen
beyond the house

and window. It shifts
as I do in bed
beneath the blankets,
awakened by the silence.

The snow outside
and me inside. What
was I dreaming?
Or is this the dream:

an old man in bed
hearing nothing,
waiting for the tick
of snow flakes, each

one a remembrance,
a scratching that never
enters the room
and that I long

to hear. This is a dream
not of past or present

but of the future
occurring now—

or not a dream,
but the thoughts
of an old man awake
in a dark house,

willing the furniture
to scrape against the floor,
or the faucet to drip
like a schoolboy's steps

as he makes his way
out of the dark woods,
wondering at the silence
around him, listening.

NAVEL

1.

Button sewn to our skin, the thread bitten off by the eternal seamstress, the darner of celestial socks.

Sewn to our chests that way, you would think it holds body and soul together, the only button on the flesh coat.

But it's more like the flower that never bloomed nine months after it was planted—the tight, waxy petals a scar from a wound we had nothing to do with and know nothing about.

2.

Every now and then I imagine the dead lined up for as far as I can see outside a telephone booth in a railroad terminal. Everything is silent. Nothing moves. As if the dead waited endlessly for the phone to ring, part of a museum exhibit where the locomotives bulk cold and still in the background.

3.

When young we stare at ourselves in the mirror, poking and prodding it, giving it our full attention.

Later, admiring the beauty of our bodies reflected in the glass, we forget that it's there, don't even notice its mark between heart and groin.

Old, we stand with arms at our sides, staring at what we've become, the sagging belly, the flaccid breasts, and with a longing we can't understand, our eyes return to its puckered circle, the plugged connection, the scar we never understood, the waxen bud that never bloomed.

MY TRIANGLE

My triangle points downward. It resembles a diaper: the top two points are pinned at either hip and equidistant from the tip, forming the sacred triangle through which we pass into the world.

My triangle is the V in vulva, that half of David's star that pointed toward earth from the palace balcony where he stood looking down at the rooftop where Bathsheba bathed in the failing light.

My triangle is the V in void, the universe turned upside down. Its apex once balanced the evening star on the tip of its finger but now is inverted and drains the light of heaven toward the Earth.

My triangle is neither right nor wrong. It dances on the head of a pin and flies a kite in its own image as if to flout the heavens. Only when I die, will it turn its peak to the celestial world again, and, with me stretched out deep within like a broken wing or a fourth but shriveled side, will it probe the silence of the starry sky.

I HAVE LIVED LONG ENOUGH

I have lived long enough
to know that one day
the earth will forget
I am here, and will turn
from me as if I was a beggar
hot and dusty from the road.
I will be abandoned
in a marketplace by the living
who will have gone home
to lunch, leaving me
with the broken crates,
orange rinds and wilted lettuce.

This does not disturb me.
In a peculiar way
it excites me, making me
enter each new day
like a beggar in a story
who limps onto the page
from over a hill, bringing
news of miracles in other lands
and asks only that the cities
and skirted figures in his words
remain with you
in the marketplace
when he is gone.

I HAVE A TALK WITH MY BODY

Body, you've served me well —
or have I served you well?
Did you direct me to turn down
one street rather than another
and to smile or growl at whoever
was coming toward me?
Did you determine every move
I made, or thought I had,
leading me through crowds
and years, disappointments,
laughter, anger and fears
to this fixed point that was
your destination all along,
as if I was hard-brained
and wired, like the ants
hauling crumbs and leaf-bits
to their hill, or the bees forever
bustling among blossoms
in search of honey for the hive
and a queen who no more knows
why she does what she does
than they do?

                    And why were you
leading me here and there?
Why were you determined
to get us to this place? What
force was leading you?
Will I never get tired of asking
these questions, even as I approach
the moment where we
part company and, in leaving

each other, collapse to bone,
muscle and ooze that insects
and worms will suck on
until what's left of us is grains
and grittiness among the stones,
a windblown dust that will scatter
into a stranger's blinking eye
and eventually disappear?

Was that the answer all along —
that we're an insignificant mote
in a mindless round, a dance
of life and death, and what we
get out of it are the little joys
and sadnesses along the way
to where we are now?

Body,
let's stop all this conjecture.
Whether you've served me
or I've served you, or whether
something we can't fathom
has tugged us through the years
to where we are now, we've come
so long and far together, let's
stay that way, inseparable
as old friends. Let's go arm
in arm, flesh and shadow,
spirit and substance,
into the great unknown.

BEAR PRINTS

At the river's edge
bear prints in the mud.
The sharp outlines
of pad and paw,
the precisely placed
trail of footsteps
already slurring
in the brown ooze.

I had come for water,
hot on a hot day
of mountain hiking.
He had come for fish
and water too on his way
to somewhere else.

Gone now, nowhere
to be seen. Only his prints
returning to mud
or, for a time, hardening
into a brittle reminder
that he was here. Prints
like Chinese, cuneiform,
hieroglyphs, these words.

ALL OVER THE PLANET

All over the planet, fields of grass
lift quivering tongues in the moonlight.
They are a chorus singing of the bones
buried beneath them, and of the whisperings
of roots and seeds clinging to the sides of stones.
The planet vibrates with their song.
Such reverberations are our future,
all that will be remembered of us
among the gongs and cymbals of the galaxies
and the dissonant choirs of cosmic dust.

THE ROSHI'S REPLY

Dreaming? Yes, you are dreaming.
This world is a dream, but not a frivolous one.
Each of us dreams a part of this dream
which was dreamt before our parents were born,
and each of our dreams, opening ahead of us,
hollows out a little more of the universe,
until a network of paths radiates among the stars,
paths like shafts of light, like facets in a diamond.

The entrance to your path is anywhere you turn,
and each step along it as natural as breathing.
Follow this path and soon it will seem
as familiar as the garden walkway behind your home,
for you will have found your path in the original dream
where all paths are contained and revealed as One.

It is like a cut-glass bowl on a moonlit night
when we can no longer tell the sparkling container
from the glittering water it contains.
Do you see? There is nothing to get excited about.
We are talking about an ordinary glass bowl.
Just a bowl. And water, just water. And yet, and yet…

REJOICE WITH ME

Rejoice with me. I feel my face
shining behind its bones as it did
before my parents were born.
How can I describe the sensation
of sinking through one identity
after another, of endlessly falling
from one mask to the next,
my face collapsing and reappearing,
each time different yet the same.
Some faces I recognize, others
I've never seen, or have forgotten,
the one and the many, all of them
drifting off like nodes of light
among all the other nodes scattering
like fireflies throughout the universe.

MY AMBITIONS

I wanted to be
many things: athlete,
teacher, millionaire.
Now I am content
to be a cricket
in the endless plains
of the Buddha's palm.

WHAT IS ALIVE IN US

What is alive in us, what vibrates
in our animal skins, is a harp string
that is never still, a harp string
tuned to the drone of silence.
It is the single thread, the radiant filament,
that sews us to our coat of darkness,
the umbilical that holds us
to the planet each of us is
yet allows us to wander among the stars—
the guy rope that secures us
to ourselves, yet lets us venture
into the darkness all the way
to the planet of someone else.

ALL WE CAN DO

All we can do on this earth is step into the future
with a sense of the many people behind us,
the living and the dead, as if we carried our bodies
like amphorae filled with sunbeams into each new day,
continually reaching inside ourselves
to scatter golden butterflies over the land before us,
or to fling them against the night, not like tears, but like stars
that will guide those who follow across the darkness.

NOTES

The Measure, The Breath (page 24). Federico Garcia Lorca (1899–1936) was the most famous Spanish poet of the early twentieth century, as well as a world-renowned playwright and director. Early in the Spanish Civil War (1936–1939) he was dragged from his home in Granada by Franco's fascist Falangists forces and shot.

A Poem (p.25). Nauplia, ninety miles southwest of Athens, was the first capital of modern Greece after the Greeks broke away from the Turks in the early nineteenth century. Twenty-five miles away from Nauplia is the magnificent Epidaurus theater built in the 4th century B.C. and still used in the Hellenic Festival each summer. It features ancient Greek drama.

At 31 (p. 26). The names are of famous poets who died young.

Living With Su-Dong-Po (page 27). Su Dong-Po (1037–1101) was one of China's greatest poets. He lived during the Northern Sung Dynasty (960–1126) and was an important politician, calligrapher and painter. The scene imagines him at one of his several places of poilitical exile, East Slope, above the Yangtze river. The speaker, a character in one of Su's poems, recounts incidents from the poet's life.

His First Body (page 29). Luigi Pirandello (1867–1936) was a great Italian short story writer and playwright ("Six Characters In Search of An Author"). He was awarded the Nobel Prize for Literature in 1936.

This Terrible Cold (page 32). Fernando Pessoa (1888–1935) was the greatest Portugese poet and one of the most original poets of all time. He invented dozens of characters through whom he wrote. Each had a distinctive personality, history, philosophy, and poetic style.

Radio (page 37). "The Horror! The horror!" are the dying words of Kurtz, a white ivory trader stationed in Africa in the employ of a big European company, in Joseph Conrad's novella "Heart of Darkness." The phrase expresses Kurtz's realization of how close chaos is below the thin veneer of civilized life.

Summer, 1953 (page 42). The names are of the great jazz and mambo musicians who played at the many clubs on New York's Forty-Second Street in the 1940s, 50s and 60s.

The Man with The Moustache (page 51). The event took place in Croatia. "Pivo" means beer in Serbo-Croatian.

At 63 (page 55). Du Fu (712–770) is considered by many to be the greatest of all Chinese poets. He lived in the Tang Dynasty (618–907), during harrowing years of rebellion and civil war. Although his poems are personal, they vividly record his tumultuous times.

Chagall's Day (page 68). Marc Chagall (1887–1985) was the popular lyrical surrealist painter of Jewish peasant life in nineteenth and early twentieth century Russia.

Pavel Tchelitchew's "Hide and Seek" (page 69). Pavel Tchelitchew (1898–1957) was the wild neo-Romantic Surrealist painter who emigrated to Western Europe from Russia during the civil war of the 1920s wound up in the United States during World War II, and died in Italy in 1957. His "Hide and Seek" has been prominently displayed for over seventy years in New York's Museum of Modern Art.

Tchelitchew's Contradictions (page 70). Some bizarre but typical incidents from Tchelitchew's life as recorded in Parker Tyler's excellent biography of the painter, *The Divine Comedy of Pavel Tchelitchew.* Dali is Salvador Dali (1904–1989) the unabashedly self-promoting surrealist painter of the twentieth century.

The Dark Figure In The Doorway (page 71) Scanning the scene, the dark figure stands in the lighted doorway far in the background of Diego Velazquez's masterpiece "Las Meninas." Velazquez (1599–1660), a seventeenth century Spanish master, was the king's painter.

Mily Balakirev: A Life in Music (page 89). Mily Balakirev (1837–1910) was the founder and driving force behind *The Five,* a group of five Russian composers—César Cui, Aleksandr Borodin, Modest Mussorgsky, Nikolay Rimsky-Korsakov, and himself—who in the 1860s joined together in an attempt to create a truly national school of Russian music. The more cosmopolitan composer Pytor Ilch Tchalkovsky(1840–1893) opposed them, although he used many Russian folksong themes in his work.

Snapshot: John Walter Plays The Cello (page 92). John Walter is both a devoted doctor and cellist of the second half of the twentieth century. He lives in California.

"Listening To Lou Harrison's 'Suite for Violin and American Gamelan'" (page 93). Lou Harrison (1917–2003) was a great twentieth century American composer of protean talents and interests. He was fond of incorporating the music of non-western cultures into his music, particularly Javanese gamelan instruments.

The Whirling Dervish (page 100). A whirling dervish is a Muslim mystic who practices ecstatic dancing and whirling, believing that he stands between the material and cosmic worlds when he does so. The dance is part of a sacred ceremony.

My Andalusia (page 102). Andalusia is the southernmost of the seventeen autonomous communities of the Kingdom of Spain. It is home to the gypsies (Roma) and their culture, especially flamenco. The scene depicted here is more an imagined stage set than a description of its landscape and people.

Shadows (page 111). The objects on the desk are a small icon of the last recognized Russian Orthodox saint, Saint Seraphim; a painting of the legendary Daoist Chinese philosopher, Lao Tzu; and a photograph of a Greek village where a *lauto* player is about to swoon in ecstasy from the music he is making. A *lauto* is a stringed musical instrument that looks like a medieval lute with a long neck.

The Roshi's Reply (Page 123). A roshi is a spiritual leader of a group of Zen Buddhists. The word *roshi,* an honorific, means "Old Teacher" or "Old Master."

All We Can Do (page 127). An amphora (plural amphorae) is an ancient ceramic Greek jar with a tall neck, large oval body, and two handles, which resembles a human figure with arms akimbo.

Morton Marcus was the author of eleven volumes of poetry and one novel, including *The Santa Cruz Mountain Poems, Pages From A Scrapbook of Immigrants, Moments Without Names: New & Selected Prose Poems* and *Shouting Down The Silence: Verse Poems 1988–2001.* In 2007, he published a new volume of prose poems, *Pursuing The Dream Bone,* and in 2008 his literary memoirs, *Striking Through The Masks,* was published. He had more than 450 poems published in literary journals, his work was selected to appear in over 90 anthologies, and he read his poems and taught creative writing workshops at universities throughout the United States and in Europe.

Marcus taught English and film at Cabrillo College for thirty years before his retirement in 1998. In 1999, he was selected to be Santa Cruz County Artist of the Year, and in 2007 he was a recipient of a Gail Rich Award for his contributions to Santa Cruz culture. For twenty-four years, he was the co-host of *The Poetry Show,* the longest running poetry radio program in the nation. A film historian and critic as well as poet, his reviews appeared regularly in West Coast newspapers, and from 1999 to 2010 he was the co-host of a television film review show called *Cinema Scene,* which broadcast in the San Francisco Bay area and on the pod (CinemaScene.Org). His website is www.mortonmarcus.com.

Photo by Jana Marcus